The Storybook of Jesus

Short Stories from the Bible
Children & Teens Christian Books

BABY PROFESSOR
EDUCATION KIDS

Speedy Publishing LLC

40 E. Main St. #1156

Newark, DE 19711

www.speedypublishing.com

Copyright 2018

In this book, we're going to talk about the life of Jesus and the parables he told. So, let's get right to it!

Most of what we know about Jesus's life is written in four gospels of the New Testament of the Bible. These are not the only historical writings about his life, but they are the ones that give the most information. The first gospel that appears in the New Testament is the Gospel of Matthew, followed by the Gospel of Mark, then the Gospel of Luke, and then of John.

Each gospel gives a slightly different version of Jesus's life because they were written at different times. They also describe the stories that Jesus told. Jesus told these stories, which are called parables, so that the people who were following him could understand the deep spiritual meaning he was communicating to them.

THE PARABLE OF THE MUSTARD SEED

For many centuries, the Old Testament told about a savior, described as the Messiah, who would come to Earth. Jesus was Jewish, but Jewish people don't believe he was the Messiah. Christians

believe that Jesus is the Christ, which means "the anointed one." They believe that he is the Messiah of the Old Testament and that he will come to Earth again.

THE STORY OF THE BIRTH OF JESUS

Mary and Joseph were engaged to be married. Before they married, an angel came to Mary. The angel told Mary that she would soon have a baby. Mary was surprised because she hadn't married Joseph yet. The angel told her that through a miracle she would be pregnant with the Son of God and that his name would be Jesus.

Mary accepted God's will for her. When Joseph found out that Mary was going to give birth, he didn't know whether he should still marry her or not.

T hen, an angel visited him to explain that the baby that Mary was carrying in her womb was the Son of God. Joseph would be Jesus's adoptive father.

When it was about time for Mary to give birth, she and Joseph had to travel to the city of Bethlehem because it was time for them to be counted as part of the census. Mary sat on the back of a donkey and Joseph led the donkey on the journey.

When they arrived at the inn, there were no more rooms available, but the innkeeper gave them the option of staying in the stable with the livestock.

Mary gave birth to Jesus there and used cloth strips to wrap him up. She placed him in a manger filled with hay so he could sleep.

ngels visited shepherds nearby who were tending their sheep. They came to see the baby Jesus and then spread the news of his birth.

Three wise men from faraway countries had witnessed a special star in the sky. They followed it and found the baby Jesus with his parents. They offered him precious gifts.

JESUS IN THE TEMPLE AT PASSOVER

After the census was over, Mary and Joseph took the baby Jesus back to their home in the city of Nazareth in Galilee. Jesus grew up to be a strong and wise young boy.

During the Jewish festival of Passover, Mary and Joseph took Jesus on a trip to Jerusalem. They were with an entire caravan of family and friends. On the trip back, they realized he wasn't with them and they got very worried.

JESUS, AT 12 YEARS OF AGE,
TEACHING IN THE TEMPLE

They raced back to Jerusalem and looked everywhere for him, but they couldn't find him. Finally, after three days of looking for him, they found him talking to the scholars and priests in the temple. The wise men in the temple were amazed at the questions he posed and the answers he gave. Mary said to Jesus, "Your father and I have been so worried. Why did you do this to us?"

esus calmly replied to them, "Why were you seeking me? Didn't you know that I had to go to my Father's house?" His parents didn't understand his reply, but this story explains that Jesus already knew that he was God's son.

JOSEPH AND MARY LOOKING
FOR YOUNG JESUS

When Jesus grew up, he began preaching and teaching to large crowds of people who became his followers. He had a special group of twelve followers who were his close companions and were called his disciples. He performed many miracles and healed the sick. He even brought people who had died back to life.

JESUS TURNS THE WATER INTO WINE

This story is about the first of the many miracles that Jesus performed.

Jesus, a few of his disciples, and his mother went to a wedding ceremony in the city of Cana. It was the Jewish custom to serve a huge banquet for the guests at a wedding. Wine would be served with the food.

THE WATER TURNING
INTO WINE

WEDDING AT CANA

However, at this wedding, the bridegroom and the bride had run out of wine. This would have been a disgraceful humiliation for the newly married couple, so Mary, Jesus's mother, asked him if he could do something about it. He told her that his time had not yet come, but Mary went forward to tell the servants, "Do whatever task my son tells you to do."

There were six stone jars nearby that held about 30 gallons each. Jesus told the servants to fill the jars with water. Jesus performed a miracle and the water turned into the finest wine. He told the servants to pour out some of the wine and bring it to the head of the banquet.

When the head of the banquet tasted the wine, he realized it was superior to the wine they had served earlier.

He went to the bride and groom and told them that usually the best wine was served first, and then lesser wines were served after the guests had been drinking for a while. He said to them, "You have saved the best wine until last."

JESUS TELLS THE PARABLE OF THE GOOD SAMARITAN

An expert in the law asked Jesus what he needed to do in order to inherit eternal life. Jesus told him this parable to explain what it means to "love your neighbor as yourself." In the parable, Jesus used a Samaritan, because most Jewish people disliked Samaritans.

esus told the law expert:

A man was traveling from the city of Jerusalem to Jericho, but when he was on the road he was violently attacked by robbers who took his clothes and his possessions. They beat him and left him for dead as he was bleeding. A priest was traveling on the road, but when he saw the dying man, he went over on the other side of the road and continued his travels.

Then a Levite, a Jewish member of the house of Levi, passed by the man and ignored him as he went on his travels. Next, a Samaritan passed by the man. He was deeply affected by what he saw. He went to the man and bandaged up his wounds and sanitized him by pouring oil as well as wine on him.

Then, he put the man up on the donkey he was using to travel and brought him to a place of lodging. He gave the innkeeper money to take care of the man and told him that when he returned from his travels he would reimburse the innkeeper for any additional expenses.

Then, Jesus asked the man who had questioned him, "Which of these three was a neighbor to the man who had been robbed?"

The law expert replied, "The one who showed him mercy and took care of him."

Then, Jesus replied, "Go forward and do as the Good Samaritan did."

JESUS CURES THE TEN SICK MEN

As Jesus kept performing miracles of healing throughout the countryside, his fame grew. One day as he was walking through a village, ten men who were very sick began to approach him. "Master, please help us," they called out to him.

CHRIST HEALING A BLIND MAN

CURED A PARALYZED MAN
AT CAPERNAUM

Jesus said to them, "Go and show yourselves to the priest. He will be able to proclaim whether you are well once more." The men turned away from Jesus to go to the priest as he had directed them to do. On the way there, they were all cured from their illnesses.

One of the men was from a foreign land. When he looked down at himself, he saw that he didn't have an illness anymore. He changed direction to return to Jesus and began to sing praises to God as he ran back. When he got back to where Jesus was, he threw himself down on the ground and began to thank Jesus over and over again.

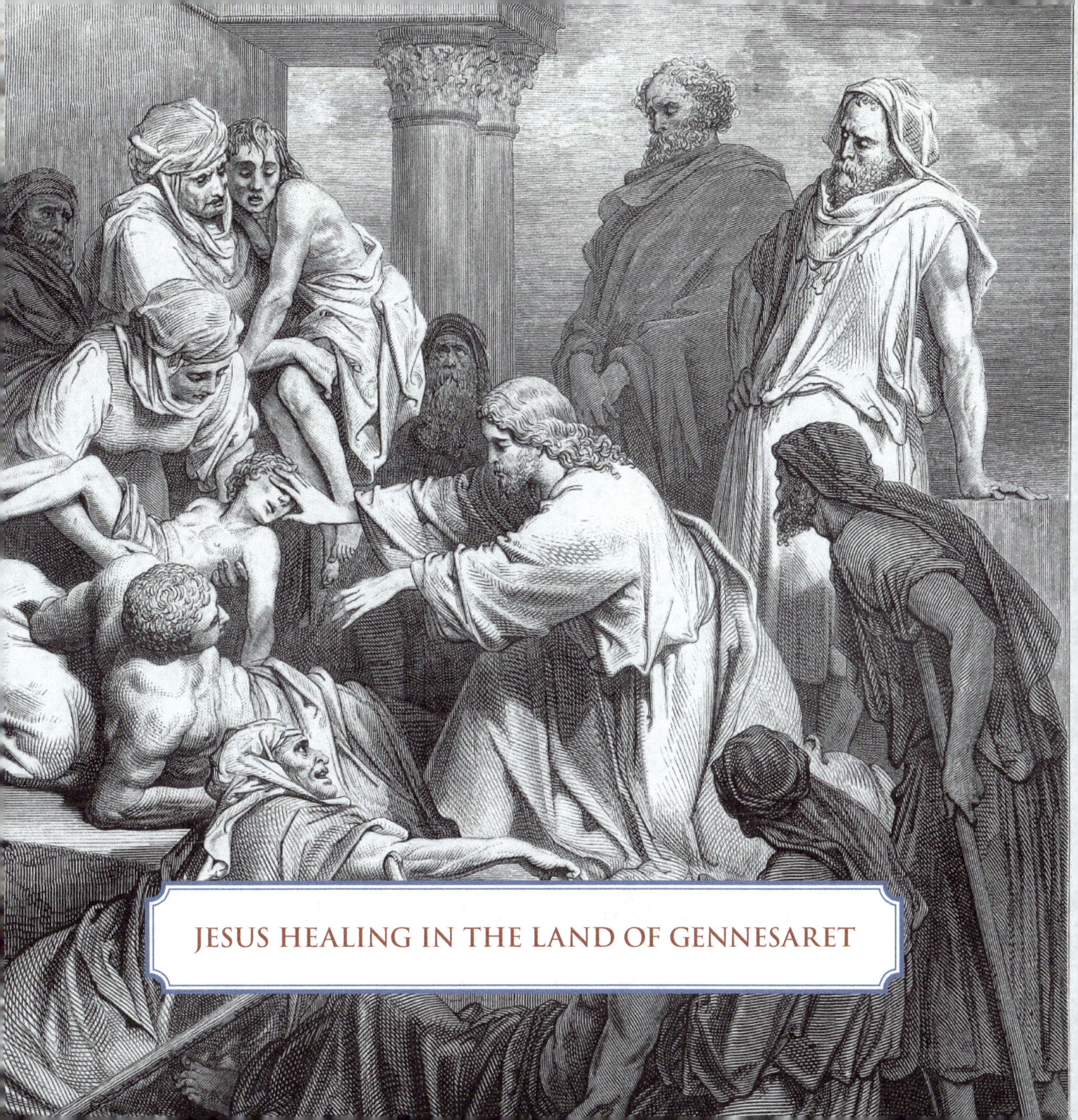

JESUS HEALING IN THE LAND OF GENNESARET

Jesus looked at him and said, "I thought that ten were healed. Where are the other nine?"

Jesus said to the man who had come back to say thank you, "Arise! Your faith has made you well."

SUMMARY

Christians believe that Jesus was and is the Son of God. They believe that Jesus Christ died for the sins of mankind. They also believe that he rose from the dead and ascended into heaven. The story of Jesus's life is told in four gospels of the New Testament. These are not the only writings about his life, but they are the ones that provide the most information not only about the history of his life but about the parables he told to his followers.

A wesome! Now that you've read about the life of Jesus, you may want to read about religious festivals around the world in the Baby Professor book:

From Islam to Christian - Religious Festivals from around the World - Religion for Kids | Children's Religion Books.

Visit
BABY PROFESSOR
EDUCATION KIDS
www.BabyProfessorBooks.com
to download Free Baby Professor eBooks
and view our catalog of new and exciting
Children's Books